CW00404944

Tips for Trips

Also available in the Classmates series:

Tips for Trips

Andy Leeder

continuum
LONDON • NEW YORK

Continuum

The Tower Building　　　　　　　　　15 East 26th Street
11 York Road　　　　　　　　　　　　New York
London SE1 7NX　　　　　　　　　　　NY 10010
www.continuumbooks.com

First published 2003

British Library Cataloguing-in-Publication Data
A catalogue record for this book is available from the British Library.

ISBN 0-8264-6471-8

Typeset by Originator Publishing Services, Gt Yarmouth
Printed in Great Britain by Biddles Ltd, Guildford and King's Lynn

Contents

v

Contents

Series Introduction

Dear Teacher

Classmates is an exciting and innovative new series developed by Continuum, and is designed to help you improve your teaching and your career.

With your huge workload, both inside and outside of school, we understand that you have less time to read around your profession. These short, pithy guides have been designed with an accessible layout so that you do not have to wade through lots of dull, heavy text to find the information you need.

All of our authors have first-hand teaching experience and have written this essential series with busy teachers in mind. Our subjects range from taking school trips (*Tips for Trips*) and dealing with parents (*Involving Parents*) to coping with the large amounts of stress in your life (*Stress Busting*) and creating more personal time for yourself (*Every Minute Counts*).

If you have practical advice that you would like to share with your fellow teachers and think that you could write a book for this series, then we would be delighted to hear from you.

We do hope that you enjoy reading our Classmates.

With very best wishes

Continuum's Education Team

P.S. Watch out for our second batch of ten Classmates, to be launched in March 2004

Introduction

The aim of *Tips for Trips* is to help teachers and governors understand the issues that need to be considered when planning educational trips. Helpful advice is offered on every aspect of the school trip, from the legal context through to practical advice on selecting students, when over-subscription is a possibility. Young teachers planning their first 'day' or 'residential' trip will find the advice particularly useful. Although this has been written based on the experience of organizing trips for students in secondary schools, most of the information contained is applicable to primary colleagues. It is recognized, however, that taking very young children out of school gives teachers additional challenges, particularly with reference to supervision and staffing ratios.

1

School Trips – A Memorable Experience

Ask any former pupil what they remember about their time at school. No doubt the idiosyncratic teacher will be high on the list, or the physical education lesson that involved a five-mile run in deep snow, or perhaps the time when the headteacher fell off the stage while taking an assembly! Alongside these memories, schools trips are bound to figure. There is no doubt that educational visits form some of the most memorable experiences of any student at school.

For the teacher they involve an enormous amount of preparation and sometimes exasperation. Until the trip is over, even the most experienced teachers will always worry that things will go wrong. When this does happen, teachers are often on the end of the 'blame culture', and certainly the expectation is that staff will fix the problem – and quickly. Those organizing the trip are answerable to parents, headteachers, governors and, in the case of tragic incidents, to the media.

So why get involved? Why add to the day-to-day pressures that face those working in the most demanding of professions? The answer is simple: it's worth it! Taking students on school trips can be the most rewarding experience; it gets to the heart of the matter. To watch students learn while having fun is why most

'To watch students learn while having fun is why most of us entered the profession.'

of us entered the profession. To develop positive relationships with young people pays huge dividends when you are back in the classroom or when you meet them while on duty in the corridor or in the playground. Those experienced in organizing school trips will know exactly what I mean, while those about to embark on their first venture may need a little more persuading, but the educational rationale is clear to see.

Governors and headteachers will expect the trip organizer to articulate and justify the trip. There may be opposition from other staff, perhaps those who teach in different departments, whose lessons will be compromised by some or all of their students being missing.

Each school trip will have its own unique aim, but underpinning all trips is a list of worthy factors:

♦ There is no doubt that they add value to the educational experience provided by schools. They provide an experience not available in the classroom.

♦ They give the teacher the opportunity to confront students with different learning challenges, which include enhancing investigative skills; problem solving; and participating in extended periods of concentrated study.

♦ Many teachers see trips as an important motivating factor, perhaps a way of overcoming barriers with pupils who show signs of disaffection. Some trips are organized on the basis of providing a reward for sustained effort or achievement in school. A fun day out can be a useful carrot for those who need special encouragement.

Tips for Trips

- They allow students to meet and work with experts who are not normally available in school time. The use of outside agencies can add enormous value to the studies being undertaken at school.

Residential trips will bring particular benefits:

- Living and working together provides students with many opportunities to develop personal and social skills.

- Relationships between teachers and students can flourish, and subsequently there are huge dividends back in school.

- Trips to different regions or countries provide students with the opportunity of meeting people from different cultures, who may speak different languages and eat different foods.

- For some students, school trips provide the only chance to visit culturally rich or scenic environments, away from their home area. It may be that the school trip triggers an aspiration to broaden horizons later in life.

If these benefits are not enough to persuade senior managers and/or governors that a particular trip is worthwhile, it is worth reminding them that school trips are perceived by parents as being an important aspect of the curriculum. The school prospectus that lists a wide range of extra curricular activities, including school trips, will be well received. Moreover, it is on school trips that the ethos of the school can be reinforced and enhanced. When trips are well organized, and when they work well, the headteacher is often on the receiving end of complimentary letters from both parents and outside agencies involved in the activity.

'There is no doubt that educational visits form some of the most memorable experiences of any student at school.'

2

The Legal Context

If the case for school trips can easily be made, all staff involved in their planning and execution must be aware of the legal context that surrounds them. Teachers should be encouraged to organize and participate in school trips, but at the same time they should recognize the responsibility that comes with ensuring that participants are safe and secure. Working with students out of school brings significant additional responsibilities.

There is a great deal of guidance available for teachers. The aim of this book is not to repeat the clear advice provided by national and local authorities, but some space is necessarily given over to the essential elements that need to be considered from the moment a school trip is suggested.

Before these essential elements are outlined, it is worth saying that no framework of regulations and guidance can provide a total guarantee of safety. Young people may meet with an accident due to circumstances that could not have been foreseen, even when very experienced leaders have followed all the correct procedures and have carried out a full risk assessment. Trip organizers can proceed with great confidence if they have followed the advice of their Local Education Authority (LEA). They should know that the vast majority of students who take part in school trips do so entirely without incident or injury.

While LEAs take the lead in publishing the regulations and guidance associated with organizing and running school trips, the Department for Education and Science (DfES) publishes a number of useful documents that provide the framework for LEA advice. The LEA document(s) and the DfES framework should be available in every school. Ideally, they should be in the hands of a senior teacher who is able to ensure that each trip complies with the regulations and guidance contained within them. The management of health and safety of visits should form part of the school's overall policy on health and safety.

Ask to see a copy of:

1. The Local Education Authority document that outlines 'Regulation and Guidance Associated with Educational Visits'.

2. The DfES document 'Health and Safety of Pupils on Educational Visits', 1998.

3. The DfES document 'Safety in Outdoor Education', 1989.

4. The DfES Circular 22/94 'Safety in Outdoor Activity Centres'.

5. The school's Health and Safety Policy.

In addition to the list above, all the professional associations provide clear advice to teachers.

These pages do not aim to address the specific issues associated with planning, organizing and participating in outdoor adventurous pursuit activities. The regulations required for such activities are rigorous. Staff participating should have special qualifications and LEAs will have very detailed mechanisms for checking staffing and facilities at named outdoor pursuit centres. In addition to the guidance offered in the documents listed above, teachers planning and participating in such adventurous pursuits must recognize the need to acquire competences from the appropriate National Governing Body (NGB). There are many of these, each specializing in a given field. Two examples include the Mountain Leader Training Board and the British Canoe Union.

Most school trips will not include any aspect of adventurous pursuit, but clear thinking is required when carrying out the initial risk assessment. An example will illustrate this point. The geography teacher planning a residential trip to Dorset, in order to study coastal geomorphology, will need to assess the risk associated with working along the coast. While the planned activity may not be deemed an adventurous pursuit, has the teacher in charge liaised with the local coastguard over tidal conditions? Are the teachers aware of the need to remind students that swimming (especially spontaneous leisure swimming) requires prior consent from parents and additional insurance? Information on risk assessment is given below.

The headteacher (and, in most LEAs, the school governors) will require a formal application to take pupils out on a school trip. It is recommended that the school adopt a standard form that covers all trips. The LEA will certainly be able to provide such a template if one does not already exist in the school. An example of a standard form is given at the end of this section.

Staff contemplating a school trip should get the tacit agreement of the headteacher *before a trip is planned* in detail. Moreover, it is certainly worth speaking to the senior teacher who organizes cover within the school. Every school can give examples of staff who have wasted time on extensive research; they may have made bookings with outside agencies/coach companies etc., but they find that their work is in vain. The planned trip may clash with another department which has organized a similar event, or an important professional development activity may be taking place, with a significant number of staff off timetable for all or part of that day. Ideally, the school should have an accurate diary or calendar of events to avoid such disappointments and clashes.

Once the tacit agreement of the head is obtained and dialogue has taken place with the senior teacher responsible for cover, the detailed research needs to be carried out. Don't be tempted to pen a letter to students/parents at this stage – you need to be certain of your facts before you reach out to your potential customers. A sensible starting point is to ask a number of questions. If the answer to any of the questions is no (or don't know), you will need to carry out more research before you move on to the stage of making a formal application to the head/governors, using the standard form available in the school.

The questions below cover the essential areas:

♦ Have I discussed the trip with the headteacher and/ or governor and gained his/her outline permission?

- Have I checked the written school procedure for arranging visits?

- Has a risk assessment been carried out (see below)?

- Do I know the procedure to ensure that adequate insurance cover is available? How much will the insurance cost? How early will I need to submit a request for insurance cover? This last point is particularly important if the trip forms part of an Activities Day, when all or most of the students are out of school. Support staff in the school office and LEA staff will need time to process large numbers of such requests.

- Will all the required forms be submitted early enough to ensure that sufficient time is left to formally approach students and parents? This is particularly important when the trip requires parents to make payments (see subsection on charging for school trips below) and/or when they need to supply medical details and/or ensure that passports are available. Foreign trips that require some or all of the students to apply for visas may need even more planning time to be built in.

- Are the planned staffing ratios adequate (see below)?

- Has the headteacher agreed to the staffing ratio?

- Have the staff who will be required to go on the trip been approached? This is often forgotten. Staff working in a large department should not be the last to find out about a trip they are expected to participate in, particularly if the trip has an early start or late return time. Has the senior teacher responsible for cover been involved in this aspect of the trip? Have support staff within the school been considered?

♦ Will there be plans to address any specific medical needs? This point will need to be reconsidered when the list of students participating has been finalized.

♦ How will the transport arrangements be secured and confirmed? This is particularly important when the school is organizing coach travel. It is easy to assume that initial quotes provided by coach companies are sufficient to secure the contract. When a range of quotes have been received and a decision made over which company to use, go back to the chosen company and get confirmation in writing. Be very clear about the times when the coach must be available and the specification required, e.g. number of seats, seat belts, toilet provision, etc.

♦ When the school minibus is to be used, is the driver qualified under LEA rules? Does the trip comply with regulations concerning the number of drivers/ distance to drive/additional non-driving adults, etc.?

Risk assessment

Although this need not be a complex process, it should be carried out before a formal application is made to the headteacher, and it should cover the areas outlined below:

- Does the trip present any specific hazards for students and staff?

- What can staff who are on the trip do to reduce the hazards to an acceptable level?

- How will the group leader ensure that the agreed safety measures are carried out by all members of staff on the trip?

- What are the procedures if an emergency arises?

- Will students and parents be aware of potential hazards, the required safety precautions and the emergency procedures?

Many factors will determine the answer to these questions not least the type of visit, the age and number of students involved, the medical/special needs of individuals participating, the location and timing of the activity, etc. For the most part, teachers will be able to carry out such a risk assessment based on existing knowledge of the location to be visited. However, there may be times when it is reasonable to ask permission to make a prior visit and assess a location, particularly if a residential trip is planned. If a travel company is being used, they are generally open to the idea of an exploratory visit: ask them!

Charging for school visits

Clear and detailed advice will be given by LEAs on this aspect. The policy outlined in each LEA document must be followed by headteachers. DfES circular 2/89

'There may be times when it is reasonable to ask permission to make a prior visit and assess a location, particularly if a residential trip is planned.'

(Education Reform Act, 1988) provides the basis for the LEA policy statements. Further details can be found in the 'good practice guide' – 'The Health and Safety of Pupils on Educational Visits', produced by the DfES and available through their publications department. Teachers may find the following checklist a useful starting point:

♦ Headteachers must not demand that parents make payments for trips that take place largely in school time; however, they can ask for voluntary contributions.

♦ The request for such voluntary contributions can exceed the cost of the trip, with a view to subsidizing those who cannot pay.

♦ Students from families who do not make voluntary contributions should not be discriminated against.

♦ Visits should be cancelled if there are not enough voluntary contributions to cover the cost of the trip.

♦ Headteachers can charge parents if the trip can be considered as an 'optional extra'. Generally, such trips will be those that do not form part of the statutory National Curriculum or those that are not set up to meet the requirements of an examination syllabus/specification. In addition, trips that fall largely outside normal school hours can attract charges. There should be no attempt to subsidize other students if the charge is made to cover the costs of an optional trip.

♦ Whatever the purpose of the trip, headteachers can ask for payments to cover costs of board and lodgings on residential trips.

Ratios

A simple rule of thumb is to ensure that ratios are high enough to ensure the safety and welfare of the students and staff participating. Guidance on ratios from the DfES is available, and the figures are given in the table below. However, all staff planning a school trip will recognize that there are many factors that will determine the final ratio agreed by the head-teacher. These will include:

♦ The specific nature of the activity to be undertaken, for example, will the larger group be sub-divided into smaller working groups, operating at some distance from each other?

♦ Do the students participating have any particular medical need?

♦ Do the students participating present any behavioural/emotional challenges?

♦ What is the academic ability of the students?

♦ What is the gender balance of students? This is a critical factor when taking students on a residential trip.

♦ How experienced/competent are the staff on the trip? This should not be under estimated. A newly qualified teacher on his/her first trip will need addi-

Table 1. DfES guidance for students of secondary age.

For day trips (e.g. to museums) within the UK	1 adult* to every 20 students
For residential trips within the UK	1 adult* to every 10 students
For all foreign trips	1 adult* to every 10 students

* Adult is considered later in this section.

tional support when working with students outside the classroom. Foreign trips, including day trips, will normally require a member of staff fluent in the language.

♦ On residential trips, the accommodation provided may give additional challenges in order to secure full supervision. Hotels/hostels may provide dispersed rooms. Other school parties may be present on site! The hotel may have paying members of the public present.

♦ Serious thought needs to be given to emergency situations, in which, for example, a member of staff needs to return home with a student, following an emergency.

Further details will be available from the LEAs who will provide schools with definite *regulations* to ensure that insurance cover is valid and appropriate. Teachers must check with their LEA: ratios will certainly be more rigorous when adventurous outdoor pursuits are planned, including swimming.

The term 'adults*' needs further consideration. In addition to the number of staff participating in the school trip, there may be regulations concerning teaching and non-teaching staff. The group leader should *always be* a teacher at the school. He/she must assume the responsibility of such a position, and other staff on the trip should recognize this. The group leader will normally be the most experienced member of teaching staff on the trip. Where large numbers of staff are required to conform to ratio requirements, it may not always be possible to use teaching staff alone. This may be a good opportunity to include support staff who work in the school. Office staff, governors, technicians and classroom teaching assistants may be delighted to be asked to go as paid or unpaid colleagues accompanying the teaching staff and students. Students will be made aware of the team effort required to run a school, and that all adults should be respected as part of this team. Experience has shown that when reaching out to non-teaching staff, be clear from the start about roles and responsibilities. Be fair to the support staff concerning their roles when sanctions have to be used; ensure that they are informed of students who may need closer supervision, because of special needs or behavioural problems. When the trip requires support staff to work longer hours than normal, be clear from the outset if they are volunteering without additional payment, or if the school will recognize the need for some additional remuneration.

When non-teaching staff form part of the team, involve them from the outset and give them as much information as you give to the other teaching staff who are participating.

There may be some occasions in secondary schools when parent volunteers may be sought to ensure

'Students will be made aware of the team effort required to run a school, and that all adults should be respected as part of this team.'

appropriate staff/student ratios. There will be mixed opinions on this. Is it fair to seek the help of a parent whose son/daughter is participating in the trip? How well do you know the parent and how might they respond when asked to apply sanctions when working with a small group of students? Is the group leader and the other teaching staff clear about the specific role of the parent helper? Does the parent understand their role? Is there a need to put the role in writing? How do you secure the help of parents? Experience shows that it is best to seek out particular parents rather than send a blanket request home in the form of a letter or newsletter. It can be difficult or awkward to decline help from willing volunteers, particularly if the reason is a lack of confidence in their ability, as opposed to being overwhelmed by offers!

Finally, an important consideration is the need to ensure that some form of vetting procedure is in place before non-teaching staff are asked to take on a supervisory role. The headteacher will need to be satisfied that the non-teaching staff accompanying the trip are suitable. 'Legislation – The Education (Teachers) (Amendment) Regulations 1998', has given headteachers and LEAs the authority to check on the suitability of volunteer helpers should this be deemed necessary.

An example of a standard application form can be found on pages 24 and 25. This can be used if the LEA does not provide a standard form. A separate form will be required if the trip involves any outdoor adventurous activity. Liaison must take place directly with the LEA adviser before adventurous activities are considered.

'When non-teaching staff form part of the team, involve them from the outset and give them as much information as you give to the other teaching staff who are participating.'

Standard High School

An application for the approval of an educational visit.

(This form should not be used if an outdoor adventurous activity forms part of the proposed trip.)

Please complete all relevant sections and submit this form at least six weeks before the proposed visit.

1. Place(s) to be visited

   _____

2. Date(s)

   _____/_____

3. Departure time_____ Return time_____

4. Transport details (name of coach hire? school minibus?)

   _____

5. Name of travel company and telephone number (if applicable)

   _____

6. Staffing (indicate group leader – GL, minibus driver(s) – MB and non-teaching staff – NT)

   _____

   _____

   _____

7. Students

   Age range: _____

   Number: Boys _____ Girls _____ Total _____

   Ratio: _____

8. Insurance: Give details of the level of cover and the company providing cover (include details even if the LEA insurance is being used).

_____

_____

_____

9. Finance: Include details of cost per student and source of funding (where parental contributions are required, please ensure that wording follows the school guidelines).

_____

_____

10. Activities: Ensure that a risk assessment has been carried out before completing this section.

Learning objectives?

Prior knowledge? _____

Any hazards? _____

Accommodation issues? _____

_____

_____

_____

_____

_____

_____

To be completed by the headteacher. The details presented satisfy the school and LEA requirements and the trip has been approved. No details should subsequently be changed without prior approval.

Signed:_____ (Headteacher) Date:_____

Tips for Trips

Action required by the group leader:

♦ Copies of this approval should be held by the head-teacher/school office/LEA/group leader.

♦ Correspondence with parents should be approved by the headteacher in the first instance. This includes letters asking for consent, contributions and letters giving details of the final itinerary.

♦ Emergency contact details should be left with the school office and at least one senior teacher.

♦ The final list of group members and a contact telephone number must be left with the school office before departure.

3

Promoting the Trip

This section looks at the need to promote and publicize the trip, from the obvious starting point when launch letters are sent to parents, through to the time when further information is sent home, (mainly when residential trips are planned or when day trips involve the dissemination of further information). It also considers the need to publicize the trip within the school, and the advantages of informing outside agencies of the proposal. In addition, the need to give individual teachers a sound starting point by developing a whole school strategy on trips is explored.

Promoting any trip will largely revolve around communicating with parents, particularly in the period leading up to the trip. Alongside the submission of the formal proposal to the headteacher, staff organizing the trip will need to pay early attention to how and when they intend to reach out to parents. Although such deliberations need early consideration, no attempt should be made to contact the parents until permission from the headteacher has been gained, and those who are organizing it are confident that the trip is viable subject to recruiting enough students. There are too many embarrassing examples where letters sent home promise an exciting school trip, planned for a specific day/week, only to find that the trip is postponed or cancelled, or that significant changes have to be made. Experience shows that those organizing the trip should be confident that their initial planning is foolproof before the formal letter to parents is sent out. This is particularly important when parents are charged for activities (see below). Parents need to have confidence in the staff planning the trip, they need to know that the planning is sound and that the logistics have been well considered. Significant amendments at a later date undermine this confidence, particularly when residential trips are planned. Asking parents for additional contributions can be particularly embarrassing.

Clearly, the nature of the trip will determine the way that organizing staff set about promoting it to parents; there are significant differences in the way an optional residential trip should be promoted, compared to a day trip that forms part of a compulsory examination assessment. Whatever the purpose of the trip, the way it is presented to all parties involved is crucial to its ultimate success.

Publicizing a proposed trip within the school, as a means of informing other staff and colleagues, is also very important. It has already been stated that all staff participating should be fully aware of their commitment and that the senior teacher responsible for cover needs to be involved at an early stage. However, there are other essential steps to take to ensure that the trip is a success and that all staff are supportive of it. Good advice is given below; the number and range of staff who need to be informed and aware of the trip is surprisingly large.

When trips are planned as an annual event, teachers should not miss the opportunity to promote the

'Experience shows that those organizing the trip should be confident that their initial planning is foolproof before the formal letter to parents is sent out.'

following year's activity by planning a celebration event and/or by publicizing the success of a venture through the school newsletter. Maintaining momentum, by informing parents of the outcome, and by saying thank you pays huge dividends. Keeping colleagues informed of a success story enhances the corporate spirit and reduces the opposition that may stem from disrupted classes. These points are discussed further in Section 7.

Long-term planning and a whole school perspective

In good schools, parents and staff will be given early information about the trips that are offered. The school prospectus and/or the first newsletter of the year should provide readers with an indicative idea of the school trips planned. Not every trip can be included, as there are innumerable occasions when spontaneous opportunities arise, but parents like to see a measured approach to the planning of trips, across all departments and, if possible, well into the future.

We should not underestimate the commitment that parents have to make, particularly when they have a number of children in the school. We should endeavour to give them an outline of the trips likely to be offered over a five- or even seven-year period, particularly as some involve significant expense, such as ski trips. Some trips are a fixed feature of the extended curriculum offered by the school, and have become an important part of the school calendar. When the school is able to indicate proposed trips well in advance, parents feel able to make informed decisions. Early information

'Keeping colleagues informed of a success story enhances the corporate spirit.'

about indicative costs and about the students who will be eligible, can be particularly useful to them.

When a school can present this kind of information in advance, and include it alongside a list of trips that actually took place in the previous year, parents will think highly of the school. They will see and appreciate the extended opportunities available to their children, and they will be grateful for the way in which it helps them to plan ahead. They will be aware of major ventures and how these sit alongside more frequent, small-scale trips offered by a wide range of different departments within the school.

The reader will already see that the case for a teacher 'in charge of trips' can be made. Although the title of such a post may need a little work, and the headteacher may need rather more persuading that such a post is worthy of some kind of financial recognition, it is a serious point for schools to consider. School trips should generate a great deal of goodwill: but when things go wrong the goodwill can easily be lost. If they go wrong at the outset, it is difficult to retrieve the situation. Parents and students deserve some form of collective planning across the school to ensure both that individual proposals for trips do not clash, and that parents are not asked to make too many commitments within a short space of time.

Students will be quick to sign up for a range of trips, but their parents may not be so enthusiastic and may not relish having to say no. Promoting trips is a whole school issue: a teacher organizing an individual trip needs to have some understanding of the wider context before the letter outlining their specific trip is first drafted.

'When the school is able to indicate proposed trips well in advance, parents feel able to make informed decisions.'

Reaching out to parents – the launch letter

As stated at the beginning of this section, the nature of the trip planned will be the determining factor in deciding the content and the amount of detail necessary in any letter prepared for parents. Among hundreds of examples, the list below shows four very different scenarios, each requiring a very different launch letter.

Trip 1 Information is available about a compulsory fieldtrip (in school time) that forms part of the geography assessment for a GCSE course. The trip involves walking to the town centre. Only one information letter is planned, no charges will be made, but the main purpose of the letter is to seek permission from the parents.

Trip 2 Initial details about an optional midweek trip to the theatre are available, but the English teacher wants to know if the trip is viable in terms of numbers of students. Students would not arrive back to the school until after midnight. The trip could not go ahead unless enough students sign up (travel cost and group booking conditions apply).

Trip 3 The history department plan to run a four-day residential trip to northern France to study World War I battlefields. Large numbers of students study history but only 40 places are available, the trip is likely to be over-subscribed. The school intends to use a travel company for all aspects of the trip.

Trip 4 The art department has the opportunity to take

all ten of its A level students to Cornwall for a week. They will be working with an artist in residence and although fees will be kept to a minimum, accommodation and travel will require significant contributions from parents. Some of the students have job commitments. Such opportunities are rare and the department is very keen to recruit all ten students for the trip.

A good starting point is to think as a parent. What information would you want if the school was informing you (or asking your permission) about taking your son/daughter out of school? If the launch letter is to inform parents about an ambitious trip (e.g. in terms of cost/duration/logistics, etc.), parents would expect fairly detailed information. If the proposed trip is modest, and the main purpose of the letter is simply to get parental permission, limited details are sufficient. However, even with the most modest of trips, parents expect to be reassured that the expedition is worthwhile and that their son's/daughter's well-being is assured. The following checklist should be considered for all launch letters, although the amount of detail on each point will vary depending on the nature of the trip. For more ambitious trips (or when some form of selection has to take place), the launch letter should make it clear that further details will follow in a later communication.

The checklist is as follows:

- *The purpose of the trip* Always start with this, parents want to know how the trip will relate to

'A good starting points is to think as a parent about what information you would want.'

schoolwork and in what ways it will enhance learning.

♦ *Departure/arrival details*　For day trips, in school time, there will probably not be any issues, but still make it clear. Students may have a medical appointment, or another commitment. For trips starting and/or ending out of normal school time, and certainly for residential trips, there may be a need to consider transport or work-related issues (for the parent and the student). Always cover yourself by stating that arrival times are approximate and are subject to traffic conditions.

♦ *Transport arrangements*　Give brief details about the mode of transport to be used.

♦ *Accommodation (if applicable)*　Even in launch letters, parents want to know a little about the kind of accommodation planned. It is worth stating in the launch letter that more details will follow in subsequent communications. Parents and students are often more anxious about this element of the trip than any other.

♦ *Food and drink*　Be clear about this. Is it included in the cost? Will they have to supply their own food for all/part of the trip? If food is to be purchased, how much money will students need?

♦ *Clothing*　Will school uniform/the school dress code be enforced? Is any special clothing required? Will the trip still take place if it is cold and wet?

♦ *Itinerary (if applicable)*　For residential trips it is worth giving brief details about some of the activities to be undertaken. Cover yourself by stating that the details are to be finalized, and that subsequent letters will give much more information, but parents will want some idea of what will happen on each day.

- *Staffing*   In the launch letter, give brief details about the staff who will be accompanying the trip. Names of staff may not be required, but reassurance on numbers and gender may pay dividends.

- *Insurance*   Make sure that any statement you make is in line with LEA policy. Trip organizers will have checked this out before submitting the trip proposal to the headteacher. Often a simple statement will suffice, such as 'cover is provided through the County's school visits and journeys insurance policy'.

- *Cost of the trip*   First, be careful with your wording here. Ensure that you follow the DfES/LEA guidelines 'Charging for School Activities' (see previous section). Parents like to know what they are getting for their money. Does the cost include transport, insurance, food/drink, entrance fee, the accommodation? Second, be clear about the logistics you intend to use in order to collect money from students. Staged payments? Cheques made payable to? Time/place for handing over monies? Third, give parents some idea about the need for spending money. Will there be any opportunities for spending pocket money? Is it possible to give parents a rough guide as to how much to take? Make it clear who has the responsibility for looking after spending money, generally this should be the responsibility of the student. For foreign trips, who has the responsibility for changing currency? Further information about spending money is given later in this section when details relating to residential trips are discussed.

♦ *Expectations*   It is always worth including a simple statement about your expectations (of behaviour) and the use of sanctions, something along the lines of: 'While participating in the trip, all students are expected to be good ambassadors for the school. The normal code of conduct, as stated in the school's behaviour policy, will apply.'

♦ *Looking after valuables*   Make it clear about your expectations over valuable items such as digital cameras, mini discs, etc. Will you allow them? Who has the responsibility over security? Items should be the responsibility of the students, but you may wish to encourage the family to take out additional insurance if the item is particularly valuable. Further consideration about taking items of value is given later in this section, when residential trips are considered.

♦ *Selection of pupils*   Some trips may be oversubscribed. Be very clear in the launch letter about your plans to select students in this event. Clarity at this point will save some difficult   telephone calls at a later date (see Section 4).

This checklist covers most standard trips. The amount of detail required will depend on the nature of the trip and the list will need to be supplemented if the trip involves any unusual activities or circumstances.

Distribution of the launch letter

When the launch letter is composed, teachers should not underestimate the time it takes to follow the school's checking procedures before it is sent to the reprographics department.

♦ A new pair of eyes often finds something to amend or add. The headteacher (or his/her senior colleague with responsibility for trips), will want to scrutinize the letter to ensure that it complies with school policies.

♦ Some thought should be given to how and when the letter is handed to students. The trip organizer will want to be confident that all the target students receive the letter. There are advantages and dis-advantages of distribution via form teachers as opposed to subject teachers. Is it best to distribute after a launch in assembly or at the end of the school day? Many of these considerations will be determined by the nature of the trip and the numbers participating. They become acutely important when over-subscription is likely and when students (and parents) are given the opportunity to complain about unfair distribution and/or unreasonable demands for the return of the reply slip.

The reply slip

The value of the reply slip cannot be overestimated. The reply slip can be used to secure essential information required by the teacher when the trip is taking place, (e.g. medical information, emergency contact numbers, etc.). It can be used as proof that parents agree to the terms and conditions of the trip. It can be a written record to confirm the payment of a deposit. As with the content of the launch letter, the details required on the reply slip will depend on the nature and complexity of the trip. Residential trips will certainly require a significant amount of information, too detailed for a reply slip. Reply slips are best kept simple.

The essential information required will include:

♦ Name of student

♦ Date

♦ Signature of parent

♦ Form/tutor group

♦ A simple statement in which the parent agrees to their son/daughter participating in the trip.

Beyond these facts, the trip organizer will need to determine if any additional information is required on the slip.

As with the timing and method of distribution of the launch letter, careful consideration needs to be given to the collection and retention of reply slips.

Has enough time been allowed between the distribution of the letter and the deadline to return the reply slip?

Decide who will collect the reply slip. There are advantages and disadvantages to using form tutors/subject staff/an individual/anybody who teaches in the department.

At what time of the day and where will return slips be collected? This is very important if they are to be handed in with a deposit. There are many examples of staff losing reply slips and/or money/cheques because an enthusiastic student handed them over while walking along a corridor on their way to another lesson, or when they were on duty in the playground, or were covering another lesson.

The issues are compounded and become more acute when selection of students needs to take place because the trip is over-subscribed. Students not selected will find any way to question the selection procedure.

Finally, where large numbers are involved and when several staff are involved in the trip, agree who is going to keep the collated reply slips.

Make sure that they are retained until the trip is over. It is normally only when things have gone wrong that you need to look up the emergency contact or to confirm that a parent agreed to the terms and conditions of the trip. This is the wrong time to find out that the slips were discarded when the deposits had been checked or when the final list of students had been drawn up.

Given the information above, the following pages exemplify how a teacher might compose a launch letter and a reply slip for the four trips suggested at the beginning of this section.

Tips for Trips

Launch Letter: Example 1

YEAR 10 GEOGRAPHY GCSE TRIP

Dear Parents

The geography department has planned a fieldtrip to Ipswich town centre. The aim of the trip is to collect evidence for the first assessed piece of coursework for the GCSE exam. Follow-up work will take place in class over a three-week period. The final project is worth 10 per cent of the total grade.

The fieldtrip will take place on Wednesday 1st July. Students will leave school at 9.00 a.m. and will return before 3.00 p.m. Students will work in their teaching groups, accompanied by their geography teacher and by a classroom teaching assistant. No transport will be required: the students will be collecting information as they walk into the town centre.

Please ask your son/daughter to bring a packed lunch and a drink. Students who receive a free school dinner are entitled to a packed lunch, please ask your son/daughter to see their geography teacher at least three days before the trip. School uniform should be worn. In the event of poor weather, the trip will still take place. Appropriate wet weather clothing should be worn – please check the weather forecast. A clipboard is essential.

The department will ensure that the students are covered by the standard Local Education Authority insurance scheme. The school will cover the cost of this insurance, as the trip forms an essential part of the GCSE course. A camera would be useful, but please ensure that it is covered by your family insurance policy.

Whilst participating in the trip, all students are expected to be good ambassadors for the school. The normal code of conduct, as stated in the school's behaviour policy, will apply.

Please complete the reply slip below and ask your son/daughter to return it direct to their geography teacher on or before Wednesday 24th June.

Your faithfully

Head of Geography

- -

Geography GCSE fieldtrip planned for Wednesday 1st July

Name of student: _____ Tutor group: _____

I agree to my son/daughter participating in the fieldtrip.

Signed: _____ (parent/guardian)

Launch Letter: Example 2

YEAR 9 TRIP TO THE THEATRE

Dear Parents

This letter contains information about a proposed trip to a London theatre planned for Wednesday 1st July. The trip is initially aimed at students in Year 9, but it will be opened up to others if numbers are insufficient to make the trip viable. Through a group booking, the English department has been able to secure 30 seats at the Dominium Theatre in London. The play is an adaptation of James Joyce's *Finnagens Wake*. All students in Key Stage 3 study at least two post 1914 authors, this will complement the studies undertaken in class.

The cost of the trip is £35.00. This includes entry to the theatre, travel (using a local coach company) and the standard Local Education Authority insurance. Three members of the English department will accompany students.

The coach will depart from school at 3.00 p.m. and will return at approximately 00.45 a.m. (subject to traffic conditions). It is expected that parents will make arrangements for meeting their son/daughter at the school. Students may use mobile phones to keep parents informed of the time of arrival back at school, but mobile phones are taken at the student's own risk and they must, of course, be turned off when inside the theatre.

There will be an opportunity to purchase food from a fast-food outlet, prior to arriving at the theatre, but students can bring their own food and drink if they wish.

This letter has been given out to all students in Year 9. If the trip is over-subscribed, the first 30 reply slips drawn out of a hat will be selected. A reserve list of 10 will also be drawn out. Please ask your son/daughter to return the reply slip direct to their English teacher, along with a cheque for £35.00 (payable to 'The Standard High School'), on or before Wednesday 17th June. If a draw is required, it will take place on Thursday 18th June. Unsuccessful students will have their cheques returned immediately.

School uniform is expected to be worn. Whilst participating in the trip, all students are expected to be good ambassadors for the school. The normal code of conduct, as stated in the school's behaviour policy, will apply.

- -

YEAR 9 TRIP TO THE DOMINIUM THEATRE – LONDON

Name of student: _____ Tutor group: _____

I agree to my son/daughter participating in the theatre trip planned for Wednesday 1st July.

I enclose a cheque, made payable to 'The Standard High School', to the value of £35.00.

Signed: _____ (parent/guardian)

I understand that if the trip is over-subscribed, a lottery draw will be made.

Launch Letter: Example 3

HISTORY FIELDTRIP TO NORTHERN FRANCE

Dear Parents

Your son/daughter has expressed an interest in the proposed fieldtrip to Arras, planned for October 2004. Details of the trip were explained to all students in Year 9 who have opted to study history at GCSE level in Years 10 and 11. This letter has been produced to give you the essential details of the trip, and sent out over a year in advance to help parents spread the payments over a number of months. The aim of the trip is to provide students with first-hand knowledge of two World Wars, both of which had a major impact on this area of France. Some students may be inspired to base their individual study on what they learn (although this is not compulsory), while others will use the experience to help with their creative writing, poetry and oral exercises in English GCSE.

The history department has been running this trip for many years and experience shows that the trip will be over-subscribed. If this is the case, 44 names will be drawn out of a hat, along with 5 reserves. Should a draw be necessary, it will take place one week from the return date given in this letter. If you wish your son/daughter to be considered, please return the reply slip below and attach a deposit cheque for £10. Cheques should be made payable to 'The Standard High School'. Those not successful in the draw will have their deposit cheque returned immediately.

Successful students will have their place confirmed in writing with details of the staged payment plan. Typically, students will need to pay £10 per month, over a 16-month period. Payment will be exclusively by cheque and collected by Mrs Whinney in the school office between 8.30 a.m. and 9.00 a.m. on the first Tuesday of each month. Further details will be sent in the period leading up to the trip. For the most part, letters will provide more detail on the trip, but there will be times when specific information is required (e.g. medical details/details of special diets, etc.). Parents should note that students will require their own passport for the trip and that an E111 (to assist in the provision of medical care in Europe) is essential. To help you make the decision about participation in this trip, the following details are provided. Please note, the details are subject to minor change: parents will be informed of any changes as they occur.

Dates: Depart – Friday 22nd October 2004, leaving school at 5.30 a.m.

Return – Monday 25th October 2004, arriving at approximately 8.30 p.m.

Please note – this includes three days of the Autumn half-term holiday.

Four full days are included in the itinerary, subject to minor alteration. Brief details are provided:

DAY 1 Ypres, World War I battlefields and visit to Flanders Field Museum.
DAY 2 The Somme battlefields (Beaumont Hamel and Vimmy Ridge).
DAY 3 Day trip to Paris (no work!). From Arras we take the express TGV train to Paris, before meeting our coach for a tour of the major landmarks. Significant time spent at La Defense, the Eiffel Tower and the Louvre.
DAY 4 Visit to La Coupole, a World War II German rocket station, near St Omer.

The students have been informed that the trip involves work on each day (except the Paris trip). Some of the work will be completed in the hotel.

Accommodation Will be in the Hotel Moderne in the centre of Arras. Students will be in en-suite rooms, typically housing between 2 and 4 students. Room allocation is sorted before departure. All meals will be provided (packed lunch for mid-day).

Meals in transit Students are expected to bring a packed lunch for the first day. They will be given £6.00 on the ferry for breakfast (outward journey) and £8.00 for an evening meal (homeward leg). We intend to use the P&O Stena on the Dover–Calais route.

Coach The trip is organized in conjunction with Adventure Travel Ltd. This local company has worked with the school on many previous occasions. An experienced driver accompanies the trip. A 49-seater luxury coach is provided. It includes seat belts, a toilet and air conditioning.

Insurance This is included in the cost. Cover is provided through the county's school visits and journeys insurance policy. Details of this are available on request.

Spending money With the exception of packed lunch on the first day, everything is included in the total cost of £170.00. However, there are many opportunities for students to purchase souvenirs, additional snacks and drinks. It is always difficult to estimate how much money students should take, but experience shows that £50 is a common amount. Details of the exchange of money into euros will be sent at a later date.

Valuables Any valuable items (cameras, mini discs, etc.) are carried at the students own risk, so parents may want to study their family insurance policy to ensure adequate coverage. As with spending money, valuable items are the responsibility of the student and staff on the trip will not take responsibility for looking after them.

Staff Four members of the history department (two male and two female) will accompany the students. In addition, a member of the French department will join the trip as translator. Staffing ratios are in line with the county's policy for residential trips.

Clothing School uniform need not be worn. Smart, casual clothes are ideal. Waterproofs are essential for trips to northern France in October. Some of the trips involve walking in World War I trenches which can be muddy, so appropriate shoes should be worn.

Expectations Whilst participating in the trip, all students are expected to be good ambassadors for the school. The normal code of conduct, as stated in the school's behaviour policy, will apply. Parents will appreciate that staff will apply reasonable sanctions if necessary.

Please ask your son/daughter to return the reply slip direct to their history teacher, along with a deposit cheque for £10.00 (payable to 'The Standard High School'), on or before Wednesday 17th June.

Yours faithfully

Head of History

- -

HISTORY TRIP TO NORTHERN FRANCE

Name of student: _____ Tutor group: _____

I agree to my son/daughter participating in the history trip to northern France. I enclose a deposit cheque to the value of £10.00 (payable to 'The Standard High School').

Signed: _____ (parent/guardian)

I understand that if the trip is over-subscribed, a lottery draw will be made.

Tips for Trips

Launch Letter: Example 4

RESIDENTIAL TRIP FOR YEAR 12 ARTISTS IN CORNWALL

Dear Parents

The art department would like to inform you of a rare opportunity for students who study A Level Art. A chance meeting with Tony Foster, a professional artist with a world reputation, has opened up the possibility of working with him in and around his studio in Cornwall. Tony has received a large number of awards for his portrayal of wilderness landscapes. While his specialism is working with watercolour, he would enjoy offering advice and guidance using a range of media. Tony's busy work schedule demands that we give him an early indication of our willingness to take up his offer. The art department recommends this trip to you: it will enhance and enrich the programme we offer to our students, and those who participate will gain a great deal from the trip.

The purpose of this letter is to see if the trip is viable. We would like all of the A level group to participate, but we understand that some students have commitments that they cannot break. We need at least seven students to make the trip viable. The details below will give you an outline of the financial commitment, and we also provide outline details of accommodation and travel.

Dates Saturday 7th June – Friday 13th June (note this is half-term).

Transport School minibus (this will be used throughout the week).
Accommodation Plymouth Youth Hostel (bed, breakfast and evening meal).
Insurance The standard local education authority scheme will be used.
Staffing Mr Hunt and Mrs Fitzsimmonds from the art department. Both members of staff have passed the Local Authority minibus driver assessment.
Cost We estimate that the total cost of the trip (excluding student spending money and money to purchase a snack midday, each day) will be £140.00. We would ask that the money is paid in seven installments, each of £20. If the trip proves to be viable, the first installment will be due in the first week of October.

Please ask your son/daughter to return the reply slip direct to Mr Hunt by Tuesday 14th September. You will receive confirmation of the trip by Friday 17th September. Further details giving you a detailed itinerary will be sent later this term.

Yours faithfully

Head of Art

- -

A LEVEL ART TRIP TO CORNWALL

Name of student: _____ Tutor group: _____

I agree to my son/daughter participating in the art trip to Cornwall.

Signed: _____ (parent/guardian)

I understand that the trip will only go ahead if seven students show a definite commitment.
I agree to the payment schedule, once confirmation of the trip is received.

Publicizing the trip and informing staff within the school

Careful consideration needs to be given to the list of staff who need to be informed about any school trip. The list of staff may be surprisingly long; it is likely that it will include non-teaching staff. The list will vary considerably depending on the nature of the trip: for example, an early departure and a late return time may have consequences for the school caretaker. Staff in the school canteen may need to be informed if large numbers of students are taken out. Those who work in the school reception and/or those who handle telephone calls from parents will need clear information, particularly if problems arise with the trip.

It is vital that certain key staff are on the list to be informed. They may be a key part of the team during the planning stage, and they deserve early information about the proposed trip. Good examples include staff who work in the school office and are expected to collect money from students or to organize insurance details. Don't let them be the last to know of the trip, particularly when you are expecting them to relieve you of some of the administrative burdens associated with organizing it. Don't take it for granted that a member of staff will be happy to assume the role as the school contact when the trip is away. Too often, staff are asked to take on this role *the day before the trip departs*. Will they be close to a telephone? Are they happy to deal with issues and problems? Do they know what their responsibilities will be, particularly if a problem arises?

'Don't take it for granted that a member of staff will be happy to assume the role as the school contact when the trip is away.'

The checklist below covers most scenarios. For many trips only some of those listed will need to be consulted:

Staff	Reason
Senior teacher responsible for cover	As suggested in Section 3, they can make or break the trip when it is at the earliest stage of planning. Does the trip clash with another trip involving the same students? Is a major professional activity planned for that day?
Support staff in the school office	Those collecting money should not be surprised when the first student turns up. The bursar or assistant who deals with banking and paying bills should be clear about their remit. They will offer good advice about receipts, petty cash, and money transfers. Staff who arrange insurance will need time to process the application and offer advice about risk assessment. Reception/telephone switchboard: do they know about the logistics of the trip (dates, times, etc.)? They often have to provide details to parents who have lost the information letter you spent hours producing! Do they know the name and telephone number of the contact member of staff back in school? Inevitably, they will be dealing with any issue or problem.

Who will hold the definitive list of the students who actually take part in the trip? How will this list be given to the office if the trip departs outside of the normal school day?

The school caretaker

Is there an issue about locked gates/security if the trip departs or arrives back outside school hours? Will overtime need to be paid? Who pays for it? Who will organize the parents who try to park their cars in the tight space required by the returning coach?

Is the caretaker aware of any neighbours who have, in the past, complained of noise when 100 students leave school at 5.00 a.m.? Can the neighbour be informed of the possibility of noise on a given date/time, in advance of the trip? This will pay dividends for school public relations.

School canteen staff

When large numbers of students are taken out of school for a day or a longer period, this can have a significant impact on staff working in the canteen. Generally, canteen staff are working within a tight budget. They must not find out, after preparing the normal number of meals, that a significant number of students are missing. Moreover, canteen staff may need to be consulted in advance about students who receive free school meals.

Alternative provision, such as the preparation of a packed lunch, may need to be made.

Teaching staff not going on the trip (see details below about the dividends of publicising a trip to those not directly involved)

It is standard practice to place a list of students going on a trip on the staff notice board. The list is more important than you think. It needs to be displayed at least one week in advance, to allow staff to prepare for disrupted lessons. In larger faculties, some department staff, who remain behind, may be expected to take on additional responsibilities (e.g. ensuring that cover work is set, supervising teaching groups, dealing with disciplinary issues in the absence of the Head of Department, etc.). None of these additional duties should come as a surprise or be requested the day before the trip takes place. Keep your colleagues on board.

Teaching staff who are going on the trip

I'm serious. Don't take it for granted that staff, who you work closely with, will always commit to a trip where the dates and times have been agreed in a meeting that they did not attend. This is vital when the trip requires a commitment out of normal school hours, especially residential trips or those that take place at weekends or in holiday periods.

'Don't take it for granted that staff, who you work closely with, will always commit to a trip where the dates and times have been agreed in a meeting that they did not attend.'

Heads of year/special needs staff	Always show them the list of students you intend to take. They can provide invaluable information about parental/domestic issues which may be relevant to the trip, especially if a residential trip is planned. Despite asking for medical details, students don't always give you the information you need: staff may know some important information. Particularly on residential trips, staff may find it useful to increase their knowledge of who to keep apart. Heads of year generally know more than subject staff in this respect.
The minibus co-ordinator	Whoever this is in the school, check with them that the entry in the booking diary is accurate/complete. Does a member of the PE department always take it at a time when you intend to use (but never enter it in the book)? Is an MOT/service planned for this period, but you only find out weeks after you have made your booking?
The co-ordinator of the school website	Increasingly schools use websites to inform parents of significant events. Is your trip publicized?

Tips for Trips

As the above list suggests, there are good logistical reasons for informing a wide range of staff about your trip. There are, however, other benefits to publicizing the trip, if only to appease those who find their lessons disrupted by your plans.

Staff, whose lessons are disrupted by having a significant number of students missing, may be less frustrated if they know the purpose of the trip and the benefits it will bring to the students. Section 8 will consider the importance of publicity after the trip has taken place, but ahead of the trip, schools might consider setting aside staffroom space for all letters sent home informing parents of such trips. Good communication in a school pays dividends in unexpected ways. There are occasions when there is space on a trip and an additional member of staff may get a chance to go, when there is not normally an opportunity open to them (e.g. an evening theatre trip).

Schools that publish a regular newsletter should take the opportunity to signal forthcoming trips. Parents who see a varied diet of trips will feel good about the way the school is enriching the education of its students. It is sometimes a useful source of information to parents if, for example, the trip is shown as 'open to all students in Year 8'. The letter inviting students to participate may still be in the bottom of a school bag; on second thoughts, so might the newsletter!

One final consideration concerning publicity is the involvement of outside agencies, particularly the media. As long as the trip is secure in terms of logistics, schools may find it useful to promote the enrichment work it does with students, through the local media. At

'At a time when all teachers seek good press and a positive spin on the work that they do, the media can be surprisingly supportive.'

a time when all teachers seek good press and a positive spin on the work that they do, the media can be surprisingly supportive. In the recent past, two examples serve to illustrate this point:

1. Details of a history fieldtrip were circulated to the local media. Year 8 students had been invited to participate in a day trip to the Ypres World War I battlefield, the Menin Gate and the Flanders Field Museum. The trip was one of a range of trips planned for the school's 'activities day'. With plans for the trip secure and over 100 students due to participate, the BBC local radio station asked if one of its reporters could accompany the trip. Subsequently a 30-minute programme was created, with very positive publicity for the school. The aims and objectives of the trip were explained, interviews with staff and students were broadcast and the presenter did an excellent job of promoting the importance of history in our schools. The radio documentary went on to win the local documentary award for 1998, and this in turn created additional publicity for the school.

2. A local newspaper had been covering the debate about the construction of a relief road, planned to relieve congestion away from the town-centre docks. As part of its coverage, a journalist from the paper joined A level Geography students investigating the environmental impact of three alternative routes. The subsequent report in the paper not only gave further coverage to the issue itself, but was glowing in its praise of the methodical way the students carried out their field investigation.

The headteacher and the governors were delighted at the positive publicity, and the geography department secured a strong link with the local planning office as a spin-off from the newspaper coverage.

'If there is a wide choice of staff available, consider the impact on the students left behind.'

4

Who to Take?

Many school trips are targeted at specific students and the staff who accompany them are, more often than not, self-selecting. However, there are occasions when the trip organizer needs to select students. This may arise because a wide invitation for an optional event has led to the trip being over-subscribed. Alternatively, the issue of selection may have arisen before invitations are sent out, with only selected students receiving details of a proposed trip. In addition, there are occasions when the trip organizer has the delicate task of selecting staff for the trip, when a range of options are open to him/her. This section has been included because the selection of students and/or staff can be an emotive issue. The issues can become acute if the trip is seen to be highly desirable (in the eyes of students and staff), if it is ambitious and exciting and if it is a residential trip. If selection is not handled well, there may be difficult issues to resolve. These take up time and energy when the trip organizer should be focused on the trip itself, rather than spending time appeasing those who are disappointed.

Selecting students

It goes without saying that for many trips, the aims and objectives of the trip pre-determine the students who will be going. A planned trip may be a reward for students who have worked particularly well on a project, or it may be part of the examination syllabus, where all students are involved. Two scenarios are given below where the teacher has to select students. Advice is given with a view to avoiding tension with students (and their parents) who are not selected to go on the trip.

Scenario 1

A day trip to Boulogne is planned as part of the school's 'activities day' in the summer term. One hundred and fifty students study French in Year 7, but there are only 50 spaces available on the trip. Experience shows that the trip is likely to be over-subscribed, but the languages department has not been able to book another coach due to lack of space on the cross-channel ferry. The department has decided that pre-selection of students is not an option and that an open invitation will be sent to all students in Year 7.

In the introduction to the letter, where the aims and objectives of the trip are explained, don't over-emphasize the curriculum advantages that the trip will bring. Clearly students who take part will gain from the opportunity to practice their language skills, but those who are not selected should not feel disadvantaged.

Liaise with other staff who are organizing alternative activities. It may be possible that dis-appointed students could be guaranteed a place on an alternative trip/activity. If this fall-back position is open to you, be very honest with parents in your letter. Tell them that over-subscription for the French trip is likely – parents like honesty. Tell the students and their parents why it is not possible to secure a second coach for the trip (they will ask otherwise). Give them the good news that a second choice is guaranteed to those who will be disappointed.

Don't over-sell the trip if you know that it will be over-subscribed. Play down the additional opportunities for shopping at Cité Europe. Emphasize the work required from the students, on the day and as homework after the event. Some students will find the trip a little less attractive if they know that it will create work for them!

Be very open and transparent about the selection procedure. In this case, you might declare that the letter is to be given to all Year 7 students and that a 'lottery draw' will be made in order to select students. Tell them if you intend to introduce other selection criterion (based on ability or work ethic?). Debate this with your colleagues first, and avoid it if you can: it opens up an unnecessary can of worms. It is amazing how students, who may not deserve to participate in the activity (for whatever reason) never fail to get drawn out of the hat!

Ensure that you give students time to register their interest in the trip, and avoid the first come first served scenario. Students and their parents have the right to be annoyed if they see some students being given an advantage because they have received letters ahead of others. In addition, you need to consider the student who, through no fault of their own, arrives late because of transport difficulties. Declare that the 'lottery draw' will be made a few days after the letter is sent home.

Always draw out some additional reserves (in strict order). Tell the reserves where they are on the list. You might decide to give the reserves some hope, by explaining that some of the original 50 selected may drop out, when they find that their friend isn't going after all.

Make it clear in the original letter how you intend to publicize the outcome of any 'lottery draw'. Unsuccessful students will be disappointed, so don't make it worse for them by keeping this aspect of the 'lottery draw' vague. Parents of unsuccessful students may be anxious about the return of any deposit which has been sent with the reply slip. On this point, my advice is to avoid cashing any cheques with your office staff until the draw has been made. It is easier to return the original cheque than to ask your colleague in the office to write a return cheque.

One final piece of advice is to ensure that a uniform approach is adopted across the department. Staff who break the ground rules cause untold problems for the group leader/trip organizer. Meet with all colleagues involved to decide just when the letters are to be given out, who is collecting the reply slip/deposit, and when these will be collected. Agree, as far as you are able, how to reach out to students who may be absent at the time that the trip is announced. As long as students and parents see that you have been fair and accommodating, tension should be avoided.

Scenario 2

The head of the business studies department has received an invitation to visit a local football league club. The club is happy to explain how it attempts to increase its revenue beyond the gate receipts it receives for home games. The club can accommodate up to 20 students and two members of staff. The head of department has a dilemma, as 62 students study GCSE Business Studies. The trip is likely to be very popular with most students, as it will not only help them with their studies on marketing, but the additional bonus of a tour of the ground gives added value. The department decide against a 'lottery draw', because they believe that this is an ideal opportunity to reward 20 students who have worked hard over a sustained period of time and attended all the lessons to date.

In this case, be honest with all the students who are studying the course. Explain to them that only 20 places are available (show them a copy of the letter of invitation if possible) and that it is impossible to take everyone.

If the criteria for selection includes work ethic and attendance to lessons, be up front about it. It would be politic to ensure that some of those selected are not necessarily the most able, in order to signal that work ethic is at the heart of the selection criteria. Moreover, if there is a number of teaching groups studying the subject (perhaps three in this case), select students from all three groups. This avoids the accusation that the trip organizer/head of department is favouring his/her group. There will still be some students who are bound to be disappointed and disagree with those selected. Ideally, the department will be able to appease them by offering an alternative outing at a later date.

For those selected, make it clear that they have a

responsibility to the others who are not going. A positive move would be to ask the selected students to produce an information pack or a display for the others to see. As the students will be selected based on their conscientious track record, they are likely to produce some excellent work. It may well be that the students who are not selected will be relieved that they don't have to produce an additional piece of work!

When the letter of invitation for selected students is drafted, ensure that full details are provided. The parents are likely to feel pleased that their son/daughter has been selected, and equally they will probably reinforce the need to make the most of the trip and to ensure that the follow-up work is produced to a high standard.

Report and celebrate the outcome of the trip in the school newsletter. Readers of the newsletter will respect the notion of selection based on work ethic (see Section 8).

Selecting staff

There are occasions when the trip organizer has the option to select staff for a particular trip. There are many scenarios where this could happen:

♦ The history department is organizing a weekend studying the battlefields in France. They need a French speaker and there are six to choose from.

Tips for Trips

♦ The food technology department wants to take 40 students to an exhibition in London. A significant number of students are male, but all the food technology staff are female. They need at least one male teacher to go on the trip. There are 27 available.

♦ A residential A Level Geography fieldtrip is planned. There are six different teachers who contribute to the teaching at A level. The headteacher will only allow four staff to accompany the 40 students on the trip.

♦ A member of the special needs team has the chance to take 15 reluctant learners to join a local army unit on the assault course. Some of the reluctant learners have behavioural difficulties. The headteacher has agreed that the special needs teacher can approach any two members of staff to accompany him/her on the trip.

The list is extensive and the reader will be able to think of many other scenarios in which selection of staff needs to be carried out. Each case needs to be considered individually, but teachers who have the task of selecting colleagues should be particularly aware that those not selected may be disappointed. Sensitivity is the key word, particularly if a member of staff has accompanied a trip on previous occasions and a new member of staff, joining the department, is a more obvious choice.

Here are a few factors to consider in the selection process. Most of the observations can be matched to the four scenarios given above.

Tips

Staff who are approached to accompany a trip deserve to be given the full details of their supervisory role, not just the headline news that 'we need you to make up numbers'.

For residential trips, will the member of staff selected be committed to the wider, additional responsibilities that go with corridor supervision after lights out?

Staff who are approached should ideally be prepared to get involved and show enthusiasm for the work/activities. This is particularly important if the trip is likely to involve strenuous activity, or if the student's behaviour is likely to be demanding. It also applies when students may be reluctant to complete written work as part of the trip. Select senior staff to accompany students with behavioural difficulties is obviously a temptation, but ensure that the senior staff are aware of the need to participate fully in every aspect of the trip, not just in behaviour management.

The balance of male/female staff needs to reflect the balance of students who are going. Don't underestimate the importance of this on residential trips.

If there is a wide choice of staff available, consider the impact on the students left behind. Look at timetable commitments carefully before approaching staff. Consult the senior teacher responsible for cover, who often have a different perspective from the trip organizer.

If it is obvious that a member of staff will be disappointed by not being selected, see them personally before it becomes widely known who is going on the trip. Be honest about your difficulty over selection and why you have asked someone else. The reasons are, more often than not, the right ones. A young member of staff may be asked ahead of someone who has participated before, to give them experience. Timetable commitments can be used or, in the case of the geography trip, the work to be undertaken may require a specialism within the subject. Disappointment at not being asked is softened by the personal touch. Too often, in the hectic way in which teachers work, the personal approach is forgotten.

Nearly all of the points made above apply to support staff in the school, as well as to the teaching staff. Don't forget to consider support staff for the trip. Equally, if they have helped on previous occasions, don't forget to see them personally if they are not being approached for the next occasion.

5

Using Educational Tour Companies and Foreign Travel

In this section, advice is offered to teachers who are considering using tour operators to help organize and plan a school trip. For the most part, the use of specialized tour operators will be considered when residential trips are planned. *Teachers will find the expertise they offer particularly valuable when foreign trips are proposed.* No specific travel companies are recommended in this section, but you will gather from the notes below that they should seriously be considered as an alternative to the 'do-it-yourself' (DIY) tour. Experience has shown that they very rarely let you down, and they offer competitive prices and value for money. In recent years, they have shown an increasing willingness to discuss personalized packages beyond the tours they offer in their brochures.

The key factor is generally the competitive price that they can offer per student. In my experience, this has held true over a 25-year period, and is still the case. Planning trips to a wide range of different destinations and for very different educational goals, tour companies, particularly those specializing in educational travel, seem to be able to match and often undercut a price arrived at through the DIY route. It all comes down to economies of scale. Their purchasing power with coach and ferry companies and their ability to provide cost-effective accommodation mean that an individual teacher, spending long hours on the telephone, can rarely negotiate a better deal. Moreover, the contacts they establish, particularly with transport providers, means that bookings through educational tour operators can be confirmed for specific dates very quickly, even two years in advance. Individual teachers will rarely persuade travel providers to commit (and agree the price) over a year in advance.

If cost is the key factor, don't underestimate the time DIY tours take to organize and the pressure that comes with ensuring that you have considered every angle. In these days of risk assessment (see Section 2), educational tour operators have been quick to recognize the importance of including this in the preliminary planning period. All the good companies are happy to help you shape your risk assessment document. It is in their interest that you can persuade the head and the governors that a proposed trip is viable, safe and well planned. They will certainly be able to offer local knowledge for the area to be visited, which might be a particularly welcome input if the proposed trip is somewhat distant and/or a new venture for the school.

If it has been some time since you last looked at an educational tour brochure, take the trouble to find out who, in your school, is the person responsible for keeping them. Locating them might be difficult because they are often addressed to the Head of Geography who left ten years ago. Persevere, and check in the most cluttered pigeonhole, the one that never seems to be emptied: the search will be worth it. In recent years, the brochures have become much

'All the good companies are happy to help you shape your risk assessment document. It is in their interest that you can persuade the head and the governors that a proposed trip is viable, safe and well planned.'

more informative and, in my opinion, more honest. From the details given in the front of most brochures, you will see that companies are more than happy to discuss embryonic plans over the telephone. If an ambitious tour is being considered, the company may even come to visit you at school to discuss your ideas.

If the information above gives the impression that the use of educational tour operators is to be seriously considered, it is meant to. However, before you are seduced by the glossy pictures showing groups of happy school parties standing in exotic locations, and before you succumb to the professional production techniques used by all the companies in the presentation of their brochures, step back and prepare a list of key questions. The checklist below should help. If the answer is not obvious from studying the brochure, telephone the company and ask them.

Consider how long has the company been going to the destination that you are interested in?

The experience gained by the company could be invaluable for a wide range of reasons. This might include knowing what days or weeks to avoid for 'local reasons' such as public holidays; parking and access issues and areas to avoid, and entry to generally unknown facilities which might enhance the educational experience and widen the recreational opportunities. These considerations are particularly important if the trip is a new venture for the school and if a planning trip (see below) isn't feasible. If the location is new to the tour operator, you might need some reassurance, beyond the information in the brochure that the location meets your needs.

Tip

If the trip is sold as a fully inclusive package check exactly what is included.

It is vital to read the small print. You will need to be sure that the initial letter sent to parents is honest and accurate in terms of the final cost. Will the school add additional charges to cover costs outside the package price? One aspect of a school trip where this is often an issue is the provision of food on the outward and homeward journey. The travel company is unlikely to include the provision of a meal during the outward journey. Are the students expected to purchase a meal and a drink from their own funds? Will the school hand out cash to students (in the appropriate currency), or is there a clear expectation that the students should bring a packed lunch for the first day? The issue becomes acute if any of the students require regular food and drink, for example if they are diabetic. For the party, as a whole, are drinks provided with each meal at the hotel/hostel, and are packed lunches provided?

Does the package cost cover the cost of entrance to museums, etc.? The company may have organized the schedule, including booking a space at a museum, but will the school have to pay the entrance fee on arrival?

Does the package price include any additional insurance premium should the school wish to provide extra cover on top of any LEA scheme? While on the topic of additional insurance, be ready to supply details of the cover provided to any parent who wishes to read the small print.

The package is certain to include accommodation, but what kind? Ask for specific details at an early stage of negotiation. When rooming is finally sorted, just before departure or on arrival, there should be no surprises. How many students/staff to a room? Will students be expected to share a double bed (which is not uncommon in France)? Are toilet and bathroom facilities shared or are they en suite? Is the hotel in a city centre location? There may be issues of noise or security to consider. How are staff to be accommodated, i.e. how many rooms are allocated to them and where are these situated in relation to the students (vital for reasons of supervision)?

Tip

Establish how many 'free places' are available for staff?

Depending on the total size of the party, the length of stay, the quality of the accommodation required, etc., 'free places' tend to be in the ratio of 1:8 or 1:6. Problems can occur if students withdraw at a late stage: will the company honour the original ratios agreed at the outset? Some companies may be prepared to negotiate additional 'free spaces' if the group size is particularly large and/or the school books the same trip over consecutive weeks or weekends for different cohorts.

In addition to the provision of 'free places', does the company offer any discounts for family members accompanying teachers? If family concessions are available, are there different rules about the initial deposit required by the company?

Find out if the company publish a Safety Management Scheme?

Safety Management Schemes cover several aspects of the trip. Educational travel companies give very specific details in their brochures and the information provided is helpful and comprehensive. It is the duty of the LEA or governing body to advise schools about asking tour operators for a copy of their safety management system. Look for information about:

Tips for Trips

- *Initial risk assessment* Companies will help staff to complete this requirement. Moreover, they are very happy to arrange inspection-visits to the proposed location. Take advantage of this – the company will meet most of the costs (accommodation and travel). All you need to do is to plan far enough ahead to ensure that a pre-visit is timely, and that issues which may arise can be addressed before the contract is signed and initial deposits collected from students and sent to the company.

- *Pre-tour safety guide* Many companies provide teachers with an excellent, concise guide about the location to be visited. While much of the information is common sense, a clear checklist is useful. Examples of details supplied include: guidance about the use of the local language (useful phrases supplied); information about local customs (dress codes, attitudes to gender/race); local attitudes to alcohol consumption (see Section 6); safety over the consumption of drinking local tap water; telephoning from abroad (money or telecartes, using international codes and setting up mobile phones).

- *The 24-hour Emergency Assistance Programme* We all hope we never to have to use this, but the systems set up by the educational travel companies are first class. They will complement and add to the school's own procedures to ensure that emergency contact can be made effectively and efficiently. Parents want to be reassured about this more than most things. They will feel confident that the school can contact them if the need arises, and they are even more reassured if they have a contact number, should they need to contact their son/daughter in an emergency.

♦ *What checks are made on contracted coach/ferry operators?* Tragic incidents, which are fortunately very rare, have prompted the educational travel companies to make very clear statements about their relationship with contracted transport representatives. Space is given at the end of this section for advice to schools about organizing their own transport facilities, and the list below shows the essential areas checked out by the travel companies:

- seat belts conform to the current legislation (in Britain and abroad);

- drivers are experienced and work within their stated hours;

- the vehicles used are suited to the specific requirements of the tour; and

- the certificates of insurance are appropriate and up-to-date.

Tips

Find out if the company is registered with bonding bodies approved by the Department of Trade and Industry.

Part of the initial risk assessment is to check that commercial operators are reputable. All the leading companies used by schools should be registered with government-approved bonding bodies. Teachers should check that the company they intend to use is registered with ABTA (Association of British Travel Agents). This ensures that money will be refunded (including advance payments) in the case of insolvency. In addition, the costs of repatriation are met, should insolvency occur when the trip is taking place. When air travel forms part of the trip, the company should also be registered with ATOL (Air Travel Organizers' Licence).

How good are the 'educational resources' produced by the tour operator?

The provision of educational resources to support school trips has been a growth area in recent years. Although they vary from company to company in terms of quality and cost, it is certainly worth asking for sample copies well in advance of the trip. The very best resources are excellent and cover a wide range of curriculum areas such as geography, history, modern european languages and art. The majority are targeted at Key Stage 3 and Key Stage 4 students.

They have been written by teachers, for teachers, and it is clear that the authors have a good knowledge

'The very best resources are excellent and cover a wide range of curriculum areas such as geography, history, modern european languages and art.'

of the National Curriculum Programmes of Study and Attainment Targets. Most have been written for use in specific locations, where local knowledge has been used to good effect. The author has used a range of resources that have been produced to support geography and history tours. What is particularly refreshing is that the resources have been written to be truly educative. In geography, the best worksheets require an investigative/enquiry approach, where students are challenged with an assertion or hypothesis and are required to think carefully about data collection techniques. In history, they contain first-class contextual information and require the students to develop their skills of historical enquiry and historical interpretation.

Whatever the subject, teachers should avoid the need to re-invent the wheel. If the resources available from the travel companies meet your needs, save your valuable time and energy and buy them after reviewing the sample copies. If large numbers of resources are to be purchased, consideration needs to be given to the question of who should pay. Parents do not like to receive additional requests for funds, so can the cost be built into the original price quoted to parents? Will the department purchase the worksheets from their own school resources?

Section 6 explores student work expectations associated with the trip. Some of the commercial resources provide material to be used before departure and after the event. Teachers need to ensure that time is set aside for studying this before the trip and completing the follow-up work.

Do commercial companies offer any additional services to enhance the tour?

You will need to look in specific brochures to find details of additional services. The list below provides information about some that are provided:

♦ *Tour directors* Some companies provide a tour director to accompany the party. Tour directors are common on tours outside Europe. There are obvious benefits having a representative of the company with you, including the ability to speak the local language (especially for tours in Greece, Russia and the Far East). Tour directors can also provide detailed knowledge to enhance trips through their commentary and their contacts.

♦ *Evening activities* Any teacher who has taken students away on residential trips will know that the evenings present particular challenges. There is a limit to how much studying and follow-up work can be undertaken, and teachers have a duty to ensure that the students are occupied during the evenings. Some tour companies have dedicated study centres with full-time staff. In recent years, schools have been able to take advantage of a programme of evening activities in these centres which include talent shows, quizzes and team challenges.

They are run by the centre staff in conjunction with teachers. Readers should recognize that teachers remain in charge of the party during such events the centre staff do not take responsibility for the students behaviour.

♦ *Study spaces* If accommodation is in one of the dedicated study centres/hostels operated by commercial companies, there should be ample space provided for classroom-style activities. White/black-boards, overhead projectors, video recorders, computers, study tables and chairs should all be available. Check, in advance of the trip, that you are not sharing such facilities with other schools staying in the centre. If the company has arranged for accommodation in a standard hotel ask, before you depart, if the company has booked these facilities on your behalf. Are they included in the price?

♦ *Student awards* There are a few companies who offer rewards to students producing an outstanding record of their tour experience. One company even offers a digital camera to the student who produces the best video, photo, journal or essay documenting their school trip.

Teachers will debate the pros and cons of using travel companies as opposed to the DIY route. If professional companies are used, there are a few other important issues to consider about the roles and responsibilities of the group leader. Many of these issues also apply to schools who decide to organize the tour themselves.

Passports/visas

Travel companies make it very clear that it is the responsibility of the group leader to ensure that students (and accompanying staff) have valid passports on departure. The passport must also still be valid when the party is due to return! Take care to inspect passports carefully when they are handed in by the students before the trip. Remind parents, well in advance of the trip, of their responsibility to ensure that a valid passport is to hand. The government website www.ukpa.gov.uk provides teachers and parents with up-to-date information about last-minute applications and renewals. As stated earlier in this book, the initial letter sent to parents about the trip should make it clear about the need for a passport, or if the school is intending to use a collective passport.

The use of a collective passport, in the opinion of the author, is simply not worth it. Most students appear to have their own passports and so do not need to be included. The rules and regulations required to obtain a collective passport are complex, and you need quite detailed information about parents and their place and date of birth. There is also a significant time factor in obtaining the collective passport. They are not cheap, and the school will need to ensure that the cost is built into the overall cost of the trip as published to parents. The website given above will provide up-to-date details, alternatively teachers can telephone 0870 521 0410.

Particular care should be given to students who do not hold a UK passport. You need to know this far in advance of the trip, just in case there are different regulations about visas for the country to be visited.

Experience has shown that individuals who are part of the school party, but who need to apply for a visa, must take responsibility and be prepared to visit the embassy or consulate of the destination country. Cover yourself by stating this responsibility in any early correspondence with parents.

There is no need to apply for visas for the vast majority of school trips. Teachers, however, need to be aware that regulations change regularly and that the cost of visas can vary significantly (for example, Russia £30, Egypt £15, at the time of writing).

Take a photocopy of each passport (or of the collective passport) and don't forget the staff! Keep the photocopies separate from the passports. This precaution will pay dividends if a passport is lost or if a member of staff has to accompany an injured student back to the UK.

Health considerations

It is the responsibility of the group leader to ensure that all staff and students travelling have all the necessary documentation relating to health matters. There are three common areas associated with this responsibility:

1. For tours in the European Union (EU), most insurance cover states that each individual should have an E111. These ensure that students and staff are entitled to free or reduced treatment costs in EU countries. They are easily obtained from main post offices, but take care to check that students don't

hand in the *application* for the E111 as opposed to the actual stamped form; they look very similar! If students claim that they cannot get application forms, call the government freephone number 0800 555777 to have them posted to you.

2. When travelling to more exotic locations, the group leader will need to check if vaccinations are required and when they need to be organized in advance of the trip. Visit www.fco.gov.uk or telephone the Foreign Office Travel Advice Unit on 0207 008 0232.

3. Some students have very specific health requirements. Section 6 considers the responsibilities of the group leader in terms of care and medication. Teachers should recognize that travel companies do not take any specific responsibility for the care of such students.

For all issues relating to health advice, teachers should obtain a copy of leaflet T6 'Health Advice for Travellers'. This is available from all main post offices.

Behaviour of students

All the travel companies make it clear that the behaviour of the students is the responsibility of the group leader and his/her support staff. When you read the 'small print' attached to the booking conditions, the wording may appear somewhat threatening. Section 6 suggests a number of strategies that can be used by group leaders and their support staff to ensure that behaviour is managed effectively.

Poor behaviour often leads to two specific issues for the group leader to resolve:

1. Damage to the accommodation provided (broken beds and shower units are common occurrences) and damage to the coach (ripped seats, etc.). Whatever the cause of the damage, accidental or deliberate, expect to be asked to pay for all or a part of it. Each incident will need to be resolved separately, but the main advice is to hold a contingency fund, ready to pay the owner of the accommodation/coach. One of the letters sent to parents, before the trip, should outline the policy about remuneration following damage. Decide in advance if you want to go down the route of trying to get the costs back from parents (this can be time-consuming and somewhat problematic, particularly if the damage caused was the result of an over-enthusiastic group of students).

   You may decide that damage is one of those unfortunate things that is going to occur from time to time. The specific rights and wrongs will need to be investigated and appropriate sanctions used, but by building in a contingency fund (hoping never to use it), you at least have an immediate response to appease the owner. Sanctions against the student(s) may or may not include attempts to get some of the costs back, but the deterrent effect of some form of visible 'community service' will pay dividends.

2. In accommodation which is shared by other school parties or by members of the public, the problem of noise associated with poor behaviour can lead to tension. The cause and effect will be dependent

on the circumstances at the time, and the degree of the problem will be variable. Whatever the circumstances, be prepared in advance of the occurrence and to eat humble pie at the time and apologize to the complaining party. Better still get the culprit(s) to apologize on behalf of the school: they really don't like doing it. Noise management is difficult when large numbers of excited young people come together on a school trip. Talk to them in advance about the practicalities of life in a hotel (many may not have stayed in one before); explain the sanctions you will use if they let you down and work hard to keep on top of the situation when you first arrive.

In extreme cases, you need to be aware that travel companies reserve the right to ask individuals or groups to leave the accommodation. In these circumstances, the company takes no responsibility for the cost or methods by which the student is sent home. I know of only one occasion where this has happened, but when it does, it is too late to check that your systems to deal with it are adequate. The named member of staff back at school should be informed immediately. He/she should be clear about his/her role in contacting parents. Make decisive decisions about the way a member of staff is to escort the student home (mode of transport/meeting up with the parents, etc.). Ensure that your emergency contact details are accurate before departure. Keep the headteacher or the designated senior member of staff informed about the incident and the sanctions you have used. Most important of all, cover yourself by explaining to parents, in advance of the trip, that the ultimate sanction is to return students home. This should not be done in a threatening way, but softened by phrases like 'we are not expecting this to happen, but . . .'. It is best done verbally, perhaps in a pre-trip meeting. The students need to be told that you have this ultimate sanction at your disposal.

Special diets

Special diets are easily managed by the tour companies, as long as they have accurate and up-to-date information before departure. Make it clear to the students what constitutes a special diet. In my experience, some students understand this to be the time to inform you that they don't like sprouts or that they can't eat meat if it's not cooked to a cinder. Warn students who are vegetarian, that the concept is not well understood in parts of Europe (France in particular). Despite your efforts and the representation made by the travel company, they are likely to be given an omelette and salad for every meal.

Book early

A final consideration about the use of professional travel companies concerns the need to book early and the time that they require you to send initial deposits and final payment. When you organize a trip yourself, the payment schedule is largely down to you, so you can collect money up to the time you depart. This is particularly useful if the trip is expensive and you want to give the students a long period to spread their payments. Travel companies will not give you this kind of flexibility. They will expect a deposit to confirm the booking, typically £30 if the total price is £200. Most companies will then require staged payments with at least a further £80 eight weeks after the deposit is paid. The final payment is expected approximately ten weeks before departure. You can see that the payment schedule is tight, particularly if you decide to make a late booking with the company. Management of the payments from students needs to be carefully staged. Parents will want to know, in advance of making a commitment, what the payment schedule will be. A further factor is the need to build in any additional charges (for the things that the school decides to offer beyond the provision made by the company). Take care to work out these additional costs very carefully: the decision to pay for meals on the outward leg of the journey, the money required to enter a museum and the cost of prizes for the winners of the nightly trivia quiz, can easily mount up. Not only do you have to add these additional sums onto the cost charged by the company, you also need to work out a staged programme of payments to enable you to meet any bills sent in the period leading up to the trip itself.

If you negotiate any extras with the travel company, always ask for written confirmation that these have been secured. It is always difficult to argue your case with the coach driver or the hotel staff if they claim to have no knowledge of the agreement.

Organizing your own transport

When hiring a coach, group leaders should recognize that it is part of their responsibility to ensure that the operator is a reputable company. For the most part, this will not be an issue. Schools generally use an operator that is very well known to them, especially if the company offers good terms based on a loyalty agreement. If in doubt and/or when a new company promotes itself, cover yourself and contact the LEA for advice. They will know if the company has an up-to-date PSV (public service vehicle) operators' licence.

Ask the company if seat belts are available for students; the regulations require that coaches have working seat belts fitted. The regulation for buses is somewhat different. They do not legally have to have seat belts, and consequently the group leader will probably deem that they are not suitable for the transportation of students. This will definitely be the case if a long journey is required. The time to be most careful is when a school has an 'activities day'. The pressure to supply enough coaches may mean that some buses are sent as an alternative. Find out in advance if the vehicle you have hired is a coach or a bus.

6

Expectations

Behaviour

In Section 5 consideration was given to the role of the group leader, particularly when things go wrong and students have to be sent home. This is, of course, the ultimate sanction, and most school trips will take place without any need to resort to the use of sanctions. The notes below provide the reader with a list of the main issues that need to be considered before departure. They are pertinent to most school trips: day trips or residential trips, visits within the local area or visits to areas further afield.

While taking students out of school gives staff additional challenges, for the most part, the school rules relating to behaviour and discipline should be enforced. Students and their parents should know that the normal rewards and sanctions used in the school will be applied, and the students should be reminded that they are ambassadors for the school and that they must accept this responsibility. It is not unreasonable to remind them that the staff who are accompanying them need their co-operation and support if the trip is to run smoothly.

Staff going on the trip should take time to consider how they will cope with the following issues. If they are relatively inexperienced, they should ensure that senior staff are in full agreement over the way issues and problems are to be dealt with.

Smoking

Decide how staff should deal with students who are old enough to smoke. Be consistent, including the staff going on the trip. Whatever the policy, ensure that you have parental support. Most educational travel companies forbid smoking on transport and in hotels/hostels. Read the small print.

Alcohol

This is normally only an issue if sixth formers are on the trip, some of whom might be above the legal age to drink. Have a clear policy and communicate it to the students before they go. There may be a grey area when taking students to some European countries. In France, for instance, young adults aged 16 are allowed to purchase and consume beer, cider and wine (although not spirits). The students will quickly become aware of this; state your policy in advance of the trip and ensure that you have parental support. Most educational travel companies state that consumption of alcohol by students is strictly forbidden, unless staff have the written permission of parents. There may be occasions when getting this should be seriously considered, for example, when students are on exchange trips. European families regularly have wine with their meals and all the family share in this experience.

What not *to purchase*

Make a decision and communicate your views about items that you do not want students to purchase. This may apply particularly to foreign visits. Some students seem to be drawn to purchasing knives or fireworks as souvenirs. Remind students that British customs officers have very clear rules about the importation of dangerous weapons, pornography, alcohol and drugs. The whole issue of, 'you *shall not* purchase...' is a tricky one. By being up-front you may be sowing seeds in their minds. Know your students; decide if the issues need to be discussed with the whole group or with selected individuals.

Sexual behaviour

While it may be difficult/unnecessary to produce a policy statement on this, make your expectations known to the students. Your expectations will apply to boys and girls on the trip, but some schools feel that it is appropriate for a female member of staff to speak directly to girls about their dress code. This really isn't a sexist statement. They may need to be told about the unfortunate (and unfair) reputation that some British school parties have when they go abroad.

With all of these issues you may find it difficult, and perhaps unnecessary, to put your views in writing. Parents of students who are due to go on a residential trip are normally invited to a pre-trip meeting. Use this opportunity to discuss such issues. If the issues are only addressed in a public forum, always cover

'Know your students; decide if the issues need to be discussed with the whole group or with selected individuals.'

yourself by sending a formal letter home (with a reply slip), stating that the normal rewards and sanctions policy will be applied throughout the duration of the trip. Always get a signed reply to show that parents agree with this policy.

Work

Students need to be clear about your expectations over work. Some trips are set up as overtly work-focused, for example, an A Level Geography fieldtrip. Others may not involve any work at all, for example, a trip to a theme park to reward a particular group for their earlier endeavours. To avoid any tension or reaction on the trip itself, make it clear when you first launch the trip just what you will require the students to do. Advanced preparation work might be a pre-requisite. Students may need to work in the evening for a set time. They may be expected to complete work after the trip and, consequently, they will need to know your deadline.

Security

Think it through, check for the obvious things that any parent would consider and discuss this with your students. High profile and tragic incidents remind us of the need to be vigilant at all times. Your risk assessment, carried out prior to the trip, will have thrown up the main issues. The list of things to consider clearly depends on the nature of the trip that you are organizing. The list below is not meant to be exhaustive; its purpose is to prompt debate between the staff who are going on the trip.

Do students know what to do if they are separated from the rest of the group?

Are students provided with a mobile phone number for emergency use on the trip? Some schools have a 'school mobile' for emergency use. There is no expectation that staff should give out their own number.

When groups disperse make sure that the rendezvous procedures are clear.

Ensure that students understand their responsibilities over the security of valuables.

In residential accommodation, discuss any worries or concerns that you may have with the owner/manager. Particular issues could include the provision of keys, the allocation of ground-floor rooms and the presence of balconies/low windows.

In residential accommodation, inform the students of their responsibilities to lock rooms and to secure personal belongings.

Health and medication

On day and residential trips, staff will need to be fully aware of any issues relating to the health of the students under their supervision. Request details of relevant medical information in advance of the trip. Remind students and parents that you must have up-to-the-minute information prior to departure.

Make sure that all the staff on the trip read and have access to the notes you receive from parents.

Staff should hold accurate telephone numbers and emergency contact details. Are these details accessible to all members of staff on the trip?

If students need to take medication, go to some trouble to ascertain if the student is to take responsibility or if the staff are expected to play a role. If medication is to be administered by staff, ask the parents to put in writing the procedures and dose required. When students have acute needs, extensive dialogue and a home visit is advised, once all parties have agreed that the trip is a viable one for the student.

Tips for Trips

Make sure that students understand their responsibilities about health-related matters. If they feel ill, they should consult a member of staff as soon as possible. When travelling, they should not compound travel sickness problems by drinking and eating too much of the wrong food. They should appreciate the need to use sun creams and sun hats, and to keep hydrated when working outside in hot sunny weather.

7

After the Trip

Evaluation

Valuable time can be spent evaluating the strengths and weaknesses of the trip. This is particularly true if the staff plan to run similar trips in the future. It makes sense to record the things that worked well and to ensure that they are repeated; it makes even more sense to recognize when things went wrong and decide what could be done to overcome the problem. Evaluation can take many forms; staff should decide how much time they can devote to it. Take the trouble to record some observations, even if it is just on the coach going home. If the next trip is a year away, keep the notes of any evaluation meeting in a secure place. The notes will be useful when you need to do the next risk assessment, prior to launching a repeat trip. If you have used an educational travel company, expect to receive an evaluation form from their perspective. Don't bin it! They do treat your responses seriously and they will respond and react to constructive criticism.

Although the staff on the trip will have the greatest input into any evaluation procedure, don't forget to consider asking others.

Tips

The students will be able to provide you with invaluable information about their perspective of the trip. If you ask them verbally, or if you ask them to fill in a questionnaire, don't forget to phrase your questions in such a way that they give you the positives as well as the negatives.

If parents were involved in a significant way (perhaps because of the cost or the logistics of getting ready for a residential trip), ask for their views. Would they have liked more information? If so, on what aspect of the trip? Were the payment schedules helpful?

Don't forget the support staff at the school who helped you plan for the trip. Did you keep them up-to-date with your requirements (sorting out the insurance details/time and method of collection of money/paying the bills, etc.)? Were cover arrangements within the school satisfactory? This can be a very big issue if the trip involves a lot of staff from one department and they were out for several days. Were the cover materials at hand? Could the person in the department who was left behind cope with the additional pastoral and academic duties, or were they swamped?

Publicity

In Section 3, when consideration was given to promoting school trips, the value of publicity was mentioned as an aid to selling future trips. If a trip has been particularly ambitious, if there was a significant cost element, or for whatever reason, a celebration event is generally well received by parents and students. It takes time and effort to put together, but it may mean that recruitment for the following year is easier.

Parents rarely get much feedback from their son/daughter, particularly about the work element of the trip. Celebrate the work that the students produce by putting it on display. Parents will be delighted to see that their money was put to good use. They are often surprised at the complexity of the work that has been set; they are delighted and proud when they see quality work produced.

You might put together a presentation showing images of the trip with amusing anecdotes. Ask for some students to talk about their views of the trip. Although they are often nervous, if you give them a structure to work to, they can really impress their audience. More parents will attend such an event if you offer them wine and cheese! They will enjoy hearing about every aspect of the trip, and many will take the opportunity to show their appreciation of your hard work. Senior staff at the school will be delighted that you are doing your bit to publicize the school in a really positive way. Don't forget to invite them to the event, as well as the support staff in the school office.

If organizing a celebration event is much too time-consuming, don't miss out on simpler ways to publicise your work. An article in the school newsletter is a must. While you might need to use a firm editorial hand, get one of the students to write the article. They prefer it when you give them some guidance over the themes you want them to report on. If you haven't done this before, you will be impressed by the quality of their writing and their ability to be informative and amusing at the same time.

A photo-montage with a caption competition always goes down well. Intersperse the silly pictures with more serious material. If the trip was originally set up to be a working trip, you wouldn't want senior managers to think that it was all fun, fun, fun! Images of teachers often attract the most amusing captions, but be prepared to lose a little dignity. Future relationships with students are always more positive if they see that you are prepared to join in the fun.

If staff are happy with the service provided by the transport company, the museum visited and the accommodation provided (on residential trips), write to them and say so. This is actually good publicity for the school and could pay dividends in future years. Those on the receiving end of thank-you letters will talk favourably about the school to their business colleagues, friends and family.

Successful school trips are rarely forgotten by students, and can be very rewarding for staff. The effort and commitment is well worth it, but be aware of your responsibilities and the framework you are expected to work within.